This book is dedicated to anybody who has ever experienced heartbreak. It is only temporary. True love is unconditional and lasts a lifetime. When you receive it you'll know, but real love starts within. Self-love is true love. Self-love is the best love.

-D.M.

Zoning

Laying in my bed staring at the ceiling.
Oh, what a feeling,
It'll be if we
were to ride side by side in this cold world.
Be my man, and I'll be your girl.
Don't hide
No lies
Just you, and I
In this ungodly place that we can make a paradise.
Follow me.
I'll show you the world through my eyes.
Your last girl had to be blind,
because you're standing in front on me and you look so divine.
Your smile.
Your mind.
I'm looking at your soul, and I'm loving your grind.
Sugar Honey Iced Tea.
We only talked two times, what are you doing to me?
I couldn't put my finger on it if I wanted.
Every time you start talking, my minds starts zoning.

P.S… I Still Love You

Nostalgia

Let's rewind, to a simpler time.
Where I'd write you a note and it read "would you be mine?"
"Yes, no or maybe." Hurry up check a box, the anticipation it driving me crazy.
It's something about you, something amazing.
You got my hands clammy, heart pumping, eyes hazy.
I'm so infatuated with ya, sometimes I catch myself just staring at your pictures.
And I can picture me your misses.
That's only if you're with it.
So, you got to let me know.
I have options lined up but they'll never compare to you.
Tell me, what it is? The way you lick your lips got me wanting to have your kids.
We only got one life to live.
Are you going to ride for me baby?
Either you ain't, or you is.

P.S… I Still Love You

Ex

We'd put a minute in it.

Not a month, or a year. We were double digits in it.

You used to promise me forever now you're gone, and it's been a minute.

We haven't spoken in so long, because you know you did me wrong.

Now you're blowing up my phone, wish you'd just leave me alone.

But you can't because you're missing it.

Your vibe, I wasn't feeling it.

My momma had predicted it.

My high, you're steady killing it.

You're coming off delirious.

I can't believe I let you hit.

So fucking glad I called it quits.

P.S… I Still Love You

Love Crazy

He told me that he loved me, but I only heard it on a certain day.

He told me that he loved me, but he only showed it in a certain way.

He told me that he loved me when I needed it, and that's what made me stay.

When he told me he loved me, he didn't know it brightened up my day.

But you deceived me.

You told me you needed me.

And when he told me, he also said I was his whole world.

Just to turn around and catch him with another girl.

So.

I did what I had to do, for me to get through to you.

Even if it meant taking a life or two.

I gave him three years of my life, and after everything he put me through…

I guess now I know what they mean when they say,

P.S… I Still Love You

"If I can't, no one else can have you."

Futile

What am I supposed to do?
when I put all of my trust in you,
just to turn around and have you play me like a fool?
You say you're turned off because I'm "acting so aloof"
You keep thinking that I'm cheating but, where's the proof?
This relationship turned you into someone you ain't want to
But how'd you turn gangster on me when I grew up with you?
Your friends keep telling me I'm "just another jawn in your phone"
You think you king and I'm just another pawn to the throne?
You think I'm just another "vagenie" to grant all of your wishes
I told you stop comparing me to all of these other bitches
I never had your heart
And slowly we were torn apart
Now the repercussions drumming
Feelings bubbling in your stomach
The truth is out now, there's no need duck it

P.S... I Still Love You

You giving me a million and one reasons to just say fuck it

Solitary

Gave you all the love that I had and you
fucked it up
Thought I was like all these other women
You didn't know you lucked up
Now you stuck, Chuck
Remember the days that I was down?
Now I'm up
I can't keep track of all my luck
They say I'm stuck up, but when I was down, they had lucked up
Now the roles are reversed
They seem to go amuck
People talk about loyalty but give it solemnly
Your bridge's ashes in my palms
I had to let it burn slowly
No Usher Raymond
It was all bound to cave in
This bad girl did it her way
Moving mountains
Day to day
I was, in the dark
You can Hear The thump of my heart
I had rolled up all My flaws
but I needed you to spark
I can't ignite it
don't know where we could've went wrong
Just yesterday
You were on my line until the break of dawn

Amid Amor

P.S... I Still Love You

With all these big sights and these bright lights
It gets kind of lonely
Wish I had someone to come back home to at night
Wish that I... I... I...
I just wanted you to hold me
Be my big homie
I guess I wasn't enough for you
Well in this case, I was too much for you
I loved you, but the trust in you was buried so deep I couldn't touch it
Got it up for you
That's due to my pretty face but the inside had started corroding
I could not fill your happy place
And that was on me.
You told me the all of the ways you had been broken, but I couldn't see
To me you weren't broken just a bit chipped from the one that one on your shoulder
Only love you had was for marijuana
Tried hard to be your Wilhelmina Wonka but you don't like chocolate
Just all of them ones up in your pocket
Damn
Was I not good enough to call you my man?
Is your ego so motherfucking intact that we can't hold hands?
Were these bitches such an impact you can't put me up on your 'gram?
Damn
And that was on me

Amid Amor (cont'd)

Because you told me how you hurt and I couldn't see, that hurts just a word
In my position I'm fitting to calm every nerve
But you didn't want me
You confide in the hoes, your mommy and your homies,
Though they didn't know me
And that was on you
Because I told you how I hurt but I was too much for you
I trusted you
They don't even know the whole you
Just of the parts that you wanted them to
And compared to them
I'll always be at the bottom of your totem
And that was on me
Because to you love comes and goes, a life is better lived with the cash and the clothes
The weed and the hoes and that was on me

P.S… I Still Love You

20/20 hindsight

Where were you when I needed somebody?
Anybody?
You weren't checking for me
You just checked in every now and then
Because you couldn't handle being lonely
You didn't show no love
You didn't give any fucks
20/20 hindsight
You will never get it right
You're a motherfucking dub
Hold up, wait
Let me get this right?
Don't try to play me out like I'm to blame we both cried at night
Don't try to make it seem like tomorrow morning it'll be alright
Because the whole time I was loving you, you weren't riding right

20/20 hindsight (cont'd)

Gave you all of me, Whole-heartedly
That was a big mistake.
All the love I gave, you couldn't give it back
Couldn't reciprocate
Try to talk to you was like pulling teeth
Couldn't communicate
When it was said and done, I looked at you and couldn't walk away
Because our first date was like a movie scene and I needed more
And that first kiss, was what my soul had been yearning for
When I was with you, could've been anywhere and I'd feel secure
Us against the world and at any time I'd go to war
But where were you when I needed somebody? Anybody?
You weren't checking for me
You just checked in every now and then
Because you felt like being nosey
I didn't get no love
I can't give any fucks
20/20 hindsight
I will never get it right

No Love

Heartbreak's a bitch,
Fuck this shit
They don't love you no more
When you down and you broke
When you need them the most
They don't love you no more
If I witnessed love or knew what it was bet it'll feel this
Every touch
every rub
every hug
every kiss from your sweet lips
If you needed something don't hesitate
just got to ask for it
just say the word, whatever it is you know I'm down with
it
But he don't love me no more
When you down and you out
When your friends ain't around
they don't love you no more

Right There

One call and I'm right there
I'm dropping everything, pinky swear
What's the sit' baby? Truth or dare
Hit my line boy,
you know I'll come running
Wherever I'm at you know I'm coming
When I'm outside
you'll hear my speakers bumping
Just tell me what's the issue?
Here's my shoulder
Let me be your tissue
B.A.E
You know I hold it down
But when you not around
You I miss you
The Bonnie to your Clyde
Ride or die
Savannah James be my Lebron
I just want your heart and some "us" time
Teyana Taylor be my Iman
We got the world hating
Ever since we started dating
They became mad because this is so amazing
In my eyes there's a glaze and
My heart skips a beat thinking of your last name
This feeling's so insane
When it comes to my heart
I barely use my brain
No pain, no gain
No wind, no rain

Uncanny

P.S… I Still Love You

Despise
Teary eyes and faded sunshine
Empty in biology before you came into my life
Had a tissue for every issue
But you wiped away the tears
Never thought that I would miss you, damn
Thought forever you'd be my man but the tables turned
And bridges burned
Unfortunately no lesson learned
Unfortunately you, I had to earn
Even though apparently, me is what you yearned
But you lied
I cried
I yelled
Then you apologized
It's cool, Maya Angelou still I rise
Because the grass ain't always greener on the other side
Go ahead and do you I'll be alright
And even though we put in years
What you put me through
In time due
I'll recover by these heavy tears
Dreams smeared
And these empty fears

Dignity

When it's said and done
And it all trickles down
The last laugh is what I'm having now
Because you twisted my crown
I lost sight
of what was profound
So, I'm owning it
I'm standing my ground
No more looking down
No more of these frowns
And I've learned
from a girl in my town
You only put up
with what you allow
You only attract what you put out
Your energy is what's hold you down
It's holding you back
Your intuition is what keeps you intact
If you ignore it
Destruction attacks
The weight's on your back
The world is heavier than ever
Proceed with caution by any measure
Storm-trooping through any weather
Quiet storm
The soundtrack to my guilty pleasures
On repeat playing loud as ever
Anita Baker era
Then I switched it to the Mobb Deep record

Reality

I've been broken
But I've never felt the pain
All things taken
It'll never be the same
But who am I, to judge someone I never knew
It could have been you
We would've been true
The last chance you had, you blew
Missed calls and a text to my phone
You really hate the fact I left you alone
I turned your house into a home
But in the end we couldn't get along
Because you're a dog and I threw you every bone
Gave you chance after chance
In high hopes of you staying my man
Walking down the aisle hand in hand
But the bitches stayed up in your pants
Now she singing all our songs
Y'all doing our dance
Same thing, different romance
Now your boys on my line
Fending for the bromance
I keep telling them it's no chance
And they can lose my number too
In my life they got no stance
They were your friends
I'm tying up all lose ends
And to be completely honest
I will never speak to them again

French Inhale

I inhale, because sometimes I can't express the way I feel
I need to get away because I hurt and it takes time to heal
I never knew that I could be so cold-blooded and dark
I only portray what I was shown, so I lack a heart
If you knew all of me you'd understand or I'd hope you would
I can't love a man because they all hurt me but I can try. I could.
It's hard to put my all into something if I don't get 100% out
At the end of the day, I still have my doubts
I exhale, because I do care, but my affection is an empty tank.
I never had it and when I thought I did I was ridiculed now I'm blank
I just need something real, someone that won't leave me high and dry
Someone that'll make me laugh more times than he'll make me cry
I took the guts of this lifeless blunt and threw it away
Instead I filled it with optimism, chance, and pearled it the right way
May I be forgiven for what I've done in my past, I'm human, I'm not perfect.
And sooner or later someone would realize that even though I mess up, I'm worth it.

P.S… I Still Love You

Love is Blind

How do you get over someone you loved?
Their euphoric smell, the nostalgia of their touch.
You reminisce of all the times you cuddled up
Just to realize you're left on "read" and they don't give a fuck
About you
Even though a month ago they used to
They claimed they weren't ready
For a year you were going steady
Then boom
Nothing but silence in your room
Tear streams filled with gloom
Can't fall this deep already
TOO SOON, TOO SOON
Your heartbeat protrudes the quiet
You're hungry for affection
their love was your only diet
Now emotions start to riot
Combined with overthinking, insecurities, and logic
Now grab your pride and tuck it in your pocket
Through all our rights, pillow fights, gentle kisses and goodnights
I can't believe somehow you still did me wrong
But love is blind, we can't get back time, nothing wrong with
moving on

Good girl, Bad world

Being a good girl in this time?
What's the point?
When the only thing men want is a fat ass and a joint
Or the good guy's insecurities make them think we're all the same
When in reality they're the ones who play the most games
Being a "good girl" in this era is a blessing and a curse
You're like the sweetest hook but just can't seem to find a verse
You either get mistreated or constantly giving reassurance
The girl stays with the dog, the interrogations just aren't worth it
Is this "modern day" love? If so, I don't want it
I'll walk around with my head up, crown on, and flaunt it
Alone
Because I haven't found someone worthy of sharing my thrown

Never Let Me Down

You never let me down in bed
You're the best I ever had
Start at the door
We be licking
we be grinding
We be kissing
Certain spots start tingling, the only thing I was missing is you.
What do you want to do? Tonight, my only focus is on you.
Come over at nine
I'll wear that thing that you like
Just want to feel you inside, floating high on cloud nine
Loving the way that we grind, you had me waiting all night
You're the only thing on my mind.
You never let me down in bed
You're the best I ever had

Mistaken

I woke up this morning thinking I was alone

Then something inside me told me to pick up the phone

Text messages, missed phone calls, and a facetime or two

I read what you wrote and I'd never though those words would come from you

"Baby I'm sorry.

I know what I did was wrong but right now I need you to pick up the phone.

I know I messed up.

I should've never let you down.

Now I got to man up and stand my ground.

Never think I would just walk away.

You said you wanted forever and I am going to give you that day."

What is a girl to do?

When all she wants is you?

You push her away, yet still expect her to stay?

When her home turned into a house, now one of you is to move out.

How do you leave someone that you love?

P.S… I Still Love You

You know deep down he's broken your trust
Do I stay or do I go? I don't Know.

You got me

He kept me on the hotline bling
Got me wanting kids and a ring
I'm not your girl, you aren't my man
But you got me
Got me in the palm of your hand
I'm envisioning wedding bands
Some years, a couple grands
Got me wanting to call you my man
Never thought I'd want a title on this
Never would've made it official
It's something about you
Whenever you leave I miss you

Vivid Friction (explicit)

He knows what it is when I'm finished in the kitchen
I'm sitting on his face while he nibbles on my giblets
He's pulling on my thong while I'm grabbing on his britches
He's tugging on my weave when we switch up positions
Backing it up
Smack me on my ass
When you busting that nut
Don't be scared, take what you want, just get up in these guts

P.S… I Still Love You

Mental Fog

That pain cut so deep
Shit
It's seeping through
Nobody really sees it
Nobody sees the real you
Spilling all of my feelings
What does it mean?
I can finally live out my dream
I'm done now
I'll be on my way
Day-dreaming of times
Thinking of the days
Containing all my thoughts
Pushing through the pain
Smiling through my anger
Internal eye rain.

P.S... I Still Love You

If only

If I knew love could feel anything as close to this
If I knew that love was an endless warm bliss
If only I'd knew
I would have showed you too
I would've have showed the world
Made it go viral
The ones who crave love the most was raised off of survival
If only I'd known how to make them listen
Take the hate out of their hearts and let their smiles glisten
If only I knew
I would have showed you too
And maybe the world would've been a little less blue
I would've showed them all
Showed them there's more to life than what you know
And you don't have to win love by being a hoe
If only I knew how to get through
I would have showed you too

Made in the USA
Middletown, DE
01 February 2023

22740980R00017